rest
& renew

M.J. James

Rest & Renew: A 30 Day Journey to Connect with God

© 2022 by M.J. James

All rights reserved. No part of this book may be reproduced, stored in a retrieval system, or transmitted in any form or by any means – electronic, mechanical, photocopy, recording, scanning, or other – except for brief quotations in critical reviews or articles, without the prior written permission of the author.

Scripture quotations marked (NIV) are taken from the Holy Bible, New International Version®, NIV®. Copyright © 1973, 1978, 1984, 2011 by Biblica, Inc.™ Used by permission of Zondervan. All rights reserved worldwide. www.zondervan.comThe "NIV" and "New International Version" are trademarks registered in the United States Patent and Trademark Office by Biblica, Inc.™

ISBN 9798987218204 (Paperback)
ISBN 9798987218211 (eBook)

Cover design & layout by Kristi Griffith, GoThumbprint.com.

Table of Contents

Introduction 5

Day 1
Come as You Are 7

Day 2
Rest in Daily Prayer 11

Day 3
Joy 15

Day 4
Hope 19

Day 5
Renew 23

Day 6
Who Leads the Leader? 27

Day 7
Too Much 31

Inspiration
Renee Vidor 35

Day 8
Materialism 37

Day 9
Prayer 41

Day 10
Mirror 45

Day 11
Peace & Safety 49

Day 12
Lead 53

Day 13
Grief 57

Day 14
Gratitude 61

Inspiration
Toni McFadden 64

Day 15
Perfect Life 65

Day 16
Anxiety 69

Day 17
Faith 73

Day 18
Fear & Strength 77

Day 19
Walk Beside Me 81

Day 20
Worry 85

Day 21
Restore 89

Inspiration
Tami Christianson 92

Day 22
Faith in Action 93

Day 23
The Pioneer 97

Day 24
God's Will 101

Day 25
Refresh 105

Day 26
Faithfulness 109

Day 27
Patience 113

Day 28
God Provides 117

Day 29
God's Attributes 121

Day 30
Peace, Be With You 125

Inspiration
Sha Sparks 128

About the Author 129

Introduction

Years ago, I came crashing into a crossroads in my life. Stress and stress responses ruled my days. I ran from one thing to the next because I had an overwhelming sense that I was always behind everyone else. I worked too hard. I worked too much. I spread myself too thin.

"Priorities" was not a concept I embodied outside of work. Running empty from one day to the next brought me face to face with the scary realization that I was on the fast track to an early grave. I saw the faces of my children and realized I was living a life contrary to the one I wanted them to witness.

My quest of recovering from burnout was a long journey. One that I still feel I am only a few steps away from swinging back into. Prioritizing balance, for me, takes constant attention.

Maybe one day in the future it will be a strong enough habit that I will not have to focus on it so much. For now, though, the terrible habits and adrenaline-fueled overreactions that I cultivated for most of my adult life are still within sight if I look behind me.

I have outrun them, but not completely left them all behind.

I share this to say that support when setting on any journey is imperative to a successful outcome. This book is for those who are tired, stressed, overwhelmed, and burned out. This book was created specifically for you, at this precise moment in time when you need to begin to feel the connection to steadiness that is vital for your recovery journey.

For the next 30 days, I invite you to read scripture. I invite you to the shared stories within so that you know you are not alone in your struggles. I invite you to reflect upon the questions daily.

Use that time for yourself. Ask the tough questions and allow the emotions to pour out onto the pages provided. Then, add strength to your day by finishing up your daily devotional time with a prayer. The journey you set upon today is a long marathon, not a sprint. Through it know that you are supported. Grant yourself grace during this time, and remember, you are not alone.

M.J. James

1
Come as You Are

Then, because so many people were coming and going that they did not even have a chance to eat, he said to them, "Come with me by yourselves to a quiet place and get some rest."

Mark 6:31

I see you, my friend. I know you are exhausted, anxious, and stressed. I know you feel pulled in too many directions. I can see you with the weight of the world on your shoulders even as you smile with love for your family and friends. I can see that you have a hard time taking time for yourself. I can see you falling into bed each night with your mind spinning, praying for sleep, but nervous that you may not be able to shut down. I have been where you are. Sometimes, if I'm not mindful, I can find myself there again all too easily.

For the next 30 days, we will journey together to deepen our faith and introduce peace back into our lives. I invite you to come just as you are, in whatever state that may be, with no pressure or judgment. Give yourself permission to take these minutes for yourself each day, knowing that God will carry you through this journey.

Questions to Reflect On:

How does the thought of taking these minutes for yourself every day make you feel? Guilty? Happy? Excited?

What are you hoping to achieve by taking this time?

Strength for Your Day:

I invite you to pray these words out loud, "God, thank you for leading me here today. Thank you for allowing me to find a quiet place with You to rest and restore myself. I ask that you allow me to hear You over these next 30 days. Help me to understand the lessons You want me to learn. I wish to travel the path You have for me, God. Please let that journey start today. Amen."

Rest in Daily Prayer

*Come to me, all you who are weary and burdened,
and I will give you rest. Take my yoke upon you and learn from me,
for I am gentle and humble in heart, and you will find rest for your
souls. For my yoke is easy and my burden is light.*

Matthew 11:28-30

Can you remember your last vacation? Weekend away? Was it one where you relaxed? Was it one that ran you ragged? I've heard so many of my friends come back from vacation stating that they need a "vacation from their vacation." Have you felt like that?

I spoke with a friend recently, one who had been struggling with burnout. She dealt with it by planning a family trip. After hours of researching, she finally booked what she thought would be a refreshing trip. Back-to-back activities had been planned to keep the kids busy and engaged. "I want to see as much as I can," was what she expressed to me. For days, she raced from one place to the next, dragging her exhausted children behind her.

By the third day, the teenage attitude had kicked into high gear. The kids complained about everything, and my friend's temper rose. "I took all of this time to plan this trip. I filled it with things to keep us busy so they could have a great experience and all it's doing is stressing me out worse than before," she confessed in a phone call she snuck in while hiding in the bathroom of their shared hotel room.

I could feel her frustration. I understood it all too well. She had forgotten to plan for one very important thing, the thing she and her entire family needed most.

Rest. Such a small word with the ability to allow us to feel such a big thing. When was the last time you felt rested? Cared for? Comforted? For many of us racing from day to day, these are things we only feel on special occasions, and sometimes not even then. What if you cultivated the circumstances that allowed you to feel this way most of the time? How different would you feel if that were a reality?

I know that reality may be hard for you to see now, but there are many out there who have done just that. They have cultivated a restful piece to their daily lives. I don't mean bedtime. I mean a time where you replenish yourself in a refreshing, intentional way. In a way that allows you to feel restored, poured into, and energized. It takes time to cultivate this habit, but when achieved, it's worth it. Daily prayer is a big part of achieving that goal.

Questions to Reflect On:

When was the last time you felt rested?

_____
_____
_____
_____
_____
_____
_____
_____

What would it look like to cultivate a lifestyle where you feel replenished?

What would it change in your current lifestyle?

What would you need to change in order to make that a reality?

_____
_____
_____
_____
_____
_____
_____
_____

Strength for Your Day:

Today, I invite you to begin a new habit of daily prayer. A few moments to thank God for your day. A few moments to ask for a need, to vent emotion, to ask for clarity. I invite you to begin making this the way you start your day, each and every day.

3

Joy

Go, eat your food with gladness, and drink your wine with a joyful heart, for God has already approved what you do.

Ecclesiastes 9:7

Acceptance is something that we all struggle with at some point. Maybe we spent our youth struggling to fit in, or maybe we have a tough time blending into our new neighborhood. Regardless, we all understand how it feels to want to be accepted.

Isn't it something quite special that regardless of our path or how muddy we show up at the door, God still welcomes us! He still approves of us because His son has already died for our numerous sins.

If we have strayed from Him, we can be confident that He will welcome us. He will want us to smile and feel joy at the welcoming He gives us all. Yes, there is still work to be done for our redemption and healing, but that is for another moment. For now, we can be joyful that God approves us, loves us, and is welcoming us to Him, always.

Questions to Reflect On:

Have you strayed away from God?

Have you been too embarrassed to return to Him?

Do you know He is there waiting for you to turn and say, "hello?"

What would it look like if you embraced this opportunity?

How would the trajectory of your life shift if you asked Him to be present within your life once more?

Strength for Your Day:

Today, I encourage you to present yourself to the Lord. Let Him know you are here, in all of your perfect imperfection, with an open heart ready to hear news of Him. Allow the joy of this prayer to flood through you throughout your day. Let it energize your thoughts and actions with a renewing spirit. As you recognize God's energy flowing within you, walk confidently in your skin today.

4
Hope

*...but those who hope in the Lord will renew their strength.
They will soar on wings like eagles; they will run and not
grow weary; they will walk and not be faint.*

Isaiah 40:31

Where is your hope today? Are you placing it within yourself? Within a family member or friend? How about with politicians to make things better? Are you feeling weak and tired? Maybe even fearful, anxious, and worried?

Television has made it easy for us all to see so many, wonderful, and horrifying things. We're fairly immune to the way people seek out politicians in their effort to make things better.

There seems to be an organization for every cause, a piece of legislation for every perceived wrong. We've become champions of using politics to "make things better." This process can make some things better. More often than not, though, they are vassals of misplaced hope.

Instead of championing our own character to gain strength by turning our eyes upward, we instead look out at those around us whom we perceive as strong enough to get the job done for us. We scream and rally in the street, we allow businesses and towns to be destroyed in the name of justice and yet we forget to open the Bible to seek how we can renew our strength to effect real and lasting change.

We are clearly called to place our hope in the Lord. When was the last time you thought about this? When was the last time you practiced this? Not only in times of trouble, but in all that we do, we should place our hope in the Lord. It is difficult for adults to swallow the idea that we are not in control. It's difficult to swallow that those around us in positions of power are not in control.

Regardless of how hard that is to come to grips with, it's true. He empowers us with thoughts to lead, thoughts to reason, and the ability to embody some of His power here on Earth. Our strength is given and derived from God.. Seeking that strength from any other source leaves us feeling anxious, fearful, and depleted. The strength that we gain from placing our hope in the Lord is unmatched.

Questions to Reflect On:

When was the last time you fully placed your hope in the Lord?

How did that affect the outcome of what you were dealing with?

Maybe you cannot think of a time you have done this. Perhaps, then, you can think of a way to place your hope in the Lord that you can begin implementing today.

Strength for Your Day:

Think about what you are hopeful for. Have you brought that request to the Lord? Today, I invite you to pray on it. Bring your hope to the Lord, and ask for guidance if necessary. Allow Him to take control of this for you so that you may not have to carry this heavy load alone.

5

Renew

Do not conform to the pattern of this world, but be transformed by the renewing of your mind. Then you will be able to test and approve what God's will is - his good, pleasing, and perfect will.

Romans 12:2

When a woman becomes a mother, putting herself last is something that seems to develop without us even consciously thinking of it. Our baby cries in the middle of the night, and no matter how much we may need sleep, we react to what the child needs. We put our needs aside to address the needs of our children.

Over time, we adjust to this new world order, as we should. What happens, though, when we adjust so much that our reaction leads to neglect? Yes, over time, ignoring your own needs to meet those of everyone else around you will lead to neglect. This is not a problem specific to mothers. It's something every single one of us can confront at different times in our lives. We just forget to take care of ourselves. We get busy. We prioritize other things.

How do we refresh ourselves? How can we renew harmony within our own minds and bodies while simultaneously still handling all the responsibilities we have? It is difficult, especially if you have fallen into neglect. After my children were born, I went into autopilot. Their needs first, always. Then my husband's. Pretty soon, I had forgotten about myself, about things I enjoyed, liked, and aspired to.

Creating opportunities to renew and refresh myself required a lot more energy once I had allowed myself to neglect my own needs. I never set time aside for myself. I saw it as selfish. When there were only a fixed amount of hours in the day, how could I possibly spend any moment of them on myself?

A shower seemed longer than I could hope for. But this time was just a small season of my life. Instead of realizing that, I allowed that time to cultivate long-term habits of neglect. I became too "busy" focusing on not only the needs of my children but on all the things I thought I was supposed to be "busy" doing. I did not put aside time to sit and reflect, renew, and refresh with God.

Questions to Reflect On:

How have you been refreshing yourself?

Have you had a lasting restored feeling from doing that thing or do you find it short-lived?

What is a new way you can try to cultivate self-care for yourself, one that could have long-term benefits in your daily life?

Strength for Your Day:

Take some time today to renew with the Lord. Maybe try a short walk outside in the quiet. If you have small kids, and they must come with you, turn it into a game. Tell them you are on a quiet walk to count all the things you can hear along the way. Take a break every 2-5 minutes to allow them to tell you what they heard, then return to the quiet. During quiet time, pray to God. What are you feeling grateful for? What are you struggling with? Tell these things to the Lord as He walks alongside you on this quiet journey. Ask Him to renew your relationship with Him, and the one you have with yourself. This action, though it is just for you, will strengthen not only your relationship with God but also with those around you as you emerge from this practice refreshed.

6

Who Leads the Leader?

All Scripture is God-breathed and is useful for teaching, rebuking, correcting and training in righteousness so that the servant of God may be thoroughly equipped for every good work.

2 Timothy 3:16-17

It's often been said that the Bible is the greatest book ever written. Within there are stories that teach us how to live and help us obtain clarity. It gives clear definitions of right and wrong. It shows examples of trials, hardship, death, life, celebration, and beauty. It shows the roles of a husband, father, wife, mother, neighbor, and friend. Through it all, there is an unmistakable undertone of power and peace that can only be found in and through God.

When gifted with children, you automatically become a teacher. You work to present the complexities and wonders of the world in the best way you are able. You strive to create experiences and memories to cultivate a love of learning. This becomes routine to us as we work to shape the tiny humans we have been blessed with. We are called to lead in our role as adults, and it's a beautiful gift that we've been given.

While the saying, "It takes a village" is still in the know, it's not seen as often in action these days. However, adults who are around children within their communities are likewise teachers. Whether they have regular verbal interactions or just brief encounters with a wave in passing, their presence, regardless of how small, still teaches the young minds around them.

Maybe the child sees them walking their dog or mowing their grass. The child is witnessing responsibility in action. Maybe the child sees them helping a neighbor fix something, then they are witnessing kindness and skills in action. We are all teachers to those around us.

Who is teaching the teacher? Even the best teachers take time to learn new things and cultivate new skills. They continue to train throughout their teaching career. Do we do the same?

Questions to Reflect on:

Who is leading the leader?

When you are feeling weak, are you asking God to guide you to His path?

Are you trying to make the path yourself?

Where are you turning for supportive guidance and leadership?

Consider the people you go to for advice. Is their advice coming from a Godly place?

Strength for Your Day:

Today, I invite you to pray to God and ask that you be guided to the path He has for your life. Ask that He provide you clarity as you go through your day and that He places around you the voices He wishes you to hear to encourage a stronger leadership within your life.

7
Too much

For the Spirit God gave us does not make us timid but gives us power, love, and self-discipline.

2 Timothy 1:7

I can remember many times when I should have been calling out to God, asking Him for help as I juggled over-exhaustion from being spread too thin. I falsely believed that I was doing everything I was supposed to be doing, while not seeing that I was actually adding in things that were unnecessary to my responsibilities.

I lived in that space for years until I finally woke up. I was sitting in my car fighting tears from feeling like I was always short on time. I looked up and prayed. I asked Him for help and clarity. I asked that He show me what it was He wanted for me because this did not feel like it was the way. I missed my children. I was so busy racing around from work to their activities. I would leave those activities to race the kids home. We shoved dinners down with barely decent conversation around the dinner table. I felt like I was always kissing them goodbye to race to another community organization meeting, volunteer efforts, or work.

Nothing that I was spending my time on was a bad thing. In fact, I am certain God liked each and every effort individually.

It was the ratio I was living under that was the problem. It was depleting my power. How could I possibly be living with the Spirit of God within my life if I was feeling this weak constantly? I was harming my spirit by taking on all of these things regardless of my motivation in taking them on. I needed to make a change, likely more than one change. And I needed God to do it.

Questions to Reflect On:

When we are feeling empty, worn down, and exhausted, where is God? Are you seeking Him out during these times?

What is one way you can concentrate on one attribute (power, love, self-discipline) from this verse?

Are you feeling loved?

Are you living life in a self-disciplined way to protect your time and limit the distractions around you so that you can ensure to give yourself the time you need to refresh?

Are you focused on the time you need for your relationship with God? Your spouse? Your children? Your friends?

Strength for Your Day:

Let us focus on our power, our love, and our self-discipline all derived from God. Do you feel each one of these with God's presence in your life? If you do, maybe offer up a quick prayer for those who are struggling with these things today. If you do not feel these attributes, today is the day you will focus on them. Ponder these things today and choose one to work on at this moment. Call on God, and ask for His guidance, and strength as you become more mindful of these attributes and seek ways to build them up again within your life for His glory.

On the worst part of being burned out…

"The worst part of burnout and intense stress has been when I lost that feeling of desire, drive, and motivation and truly just wanted to shut down. It's a sad and empty feeling."

On walking with God…

"I cannot imagine getting through these times in my life without my Heavenly Father being my Refuge and strength. When I felt like completely shutting down or running away, I instead have given all of my anxiety, stress, and overwhelm to Him to handle, because I seriously cannot do it on my own. When I've done this, He guides me through the struggle so I come out on the other side refreshed and ready to move forward again. While I've had a relatively close relationship with God much of my life, I can honestly say that it's the high stress and times of physical, emotional, and situational burnout that have brought me closer to Him because He became all I had and my only hope. And He never disappoints."

Renee Vidor, Coach & Speaker, Founder of Winner's Circle Community, Author of *Measuring Up How to Win in a World of Comparison* | ReneeVidor.com

8

Materialism

Your beauty should not come from outward adornment, such as elaborate hairstyles and the wearing of gold jewelry or fine clothes. Rather, it should be that of your inner self, the unfading beauty of a gentle and quiet spirit, which is of great worth in God's sight.

1 Peter 3:3-4

I stood at the gleaming jewelry counter waiting for the gentleman to come back. I had held on to the rings as long as I could after he had left us. I had held out, hoping he would start to handle his financial responsibilities for the children. As much as I was working, my paycheck never seemed to stretch far enough. We had the rings appraised years ago, so I knew the diamond was worth at least a few thousand. It would be so nice to have that in the bank. I wouldn't have to keep borrowing from my parents. I could take the kids shopping for some much-needed school clothes.

I noted the kindness in the gentleman's eyes as he walked slowly toward me. Kindness, and something else…pity? "I'm so sorry to tell you this miss, but this is not a real diamond."

"What do you mean it isn't real? I was there when it was appraised, it is real."

"I don't know what happened between then and now, but this is a really nice fake."

Yes, this made sense. I was worthless, just as this ring was worthless, I thought. Worthless. It was a badge I had worn for years, and now it seemed as though that price tag had been displayed for the world to see. For how long? When had he switched the stone? Did it matter, I asked myself. I took the small amount the kind gentleman offered me for the gold rings and fake stone, and left trying desperately to hold my head up.

It took me a long time to realize that I judged my self-worth on that ring. I judged it based on what I had, or more accurately, what I did not have. I looked at others and compared myself to the materialistic things I saw around me. We tend to concentrate more on what we can see instead of on the things we cannot. Focusing on the adornments can and will only get us so far. Often, it will leave us empty.

This is not to say we cannot have nice things, but rather, that we do not let those things shape who we are. The character within us should align with whom God wants us to be, His image. For us to achieve that, we must look within to beautify and purify our inner character in order that we embody all that God has set within us.

Questions to Reflect On:

Do you set your own self-worth by comparing yourself to the things you see around you?

Do you feel inferior to others because they may outwardly "have more" or "have nicer" than you?

When was the last time you reviewed your character with the same scrutiny you use to observe the materialistic things you think are missing from your life?

If you took the time to review yourself inwardly, what would you discover?

Strength for Your Day:

Today, I urge you to look within. Is there a part of your character that you need to strengthen? Maybe you feel worthless like I once did. Maybe you see yourself talking about others too much. Maybe you snap too much at your loved ones. Today, pick one trait and ask God to guide you as you learn to strengthen that trait. Ask Him to help you reform yourself in His image so that you may align with the strength He has placed within you once more.

9

Prayer

Until now you have not asked for anything in my name. Ask and you will receive, and your joy will be complete.

John 16:24

When I was attending Catholic and Lutheran schools as an elementary student, I can remember being taught different ways to pray. In Lutheran school, there was a lot of singing. In Catholic school, there was a lot of "this is what you should ask for" direction given. A blend of both of those things has existed well into my adult life as a guide for prayer.

It wasn't until recently, however, that I learned there were many ways to pray. Many ways to bring requests and thoughts to God. Many ways to ask for what I hoped and dreamed, while simultaneously being thankful for whatever I have received. While it wasn't a new concept, it was a much deeper realm than I had been taught before.

I much prefer hearing, "Mom, can we have pancakes for dinner?" over being asked, "Mom, what's for dinner?" One of those gives me a specific idea about what they would like to eat. The other leaves me to figure it out on my own. I often think God is busy. Maybe I can make His day easier if I just ask for and thank Him for something specific, even if that's not the outcome.

My prayers now consist of something like, "God, I would really love for you to guide me in this new business venture, but please allow me to only stay on your path for my life. If that is different from what I am pursuing, please know I am open to receiving this and want only to walk on the path you have set for me. Thank you for blessing me with the surrounding opportunities. I appreciate your guidance in every area of my life."

Since I started to pray this way, I've become increasingly more mindful about what it is I am truly thinking of during prayer. It took some adjusting and time to build up to, but it's made my prayers more meaningful and less abstract. It has made me more conscious of who and what I am asking for. It's made me conscious of praying for others in a more direct way.

Questions to Reflect On:

Am I mindful when I pray, or am I just repeating the words I have been taught to say?

Do I understand the meaning behind what I am saying when I am in prayer?

How can I strengthen the significance of my relationship with God through prayer?

How will this stronger relationship affect my life?

Strength for Your Day:

Today, be specific with your prayers. Show up to God with intention and ask Him for what you wish to receive for yourself or the person you are praying for. Thank Him specifically for what you are grateful for. Try to add this practice into your prayer routine regularly.

10

Mirror

For now we see only a reflection as in a mirror; then we shall see face to face. Now I know in part; then I shall know fully, even as I am fully known.

1 Corinthians 13:12

I remember a time in my life when I avoided mirrors. It pained me to see my own face. It shamed me to see what I had become, the life I was living. I was in an unhealthy marriage trying to hold my head up while manipulation, and negativity weighed in from all sides. I never opened my Bible. Prayer for me consisted of what was done in Church each Sunday. I sat through an hour each week trying hard to appear to those around us like we were all OK.

The façade worked with those I saw once a week. That was easy. Each morning, though, I had to face myself as I brushed my teeth. I would purposefully avert my eyes. I hated everything I saw in that mirror. My outward appearance, my inward character, everything.

Years later, the circumstances of my life had changed, but I still hated my reflection. My husband had left, and I was a single mom of three children. I was on the road to divorce, which felt like the exact opposite of what God wanted even though the marriage was incredibly unhealthy and abusive. I was living with my parents, no longer living under the fear of going hungry constantly. I no longer had some of the same worries I did during my married life. There was more stability and safety now.

In many ways things were better, yet I still despised the sight of myself.

I thought it was because I had put on unhealthy weight from the cheap and over-processed food we were forced to eat for so long. I thought it was because I often lacked time to take care of my outward appearance with the kids constantly vying for my attention.

It took me quite a while to realize that what I was seeing in the mirror was the brokenness of character. It was the inside that I was reflecting outward, and it was ugly. God was not present there as He should have been. I had hidden Him. I had buried Him down, ignored Him, although I "prayed." I went to church but sat as an empty shell going through all the right motions but allowing absolutely nothing to penetrate.

I was desperately lost inside the swirl of negativity, desperation, fear, anxiety, and stress that my unhealthy and emotionally abusive marriage had bred.

Many, many bad behaviors and habits sprung from this time in my life. It took years of concentrated effort and building a relationship with God to set that all back onto God's path. I had not reflected outwardly anything related to God, but I could once more. That was the thought that struck me one day. It was the thought that encouraged me to open the Bible and just read. It was the thought that prompted me to open a devotional so that someone could lead me toward God, as I did not know the way.

Questions to Reflect On:

Do you know God as He knows you?

When you look at your reflection do you see God's love shining back out at you?

Do you see a glimpse of the beautifully crafted image of God within yourself? Or do you feel only negatively about yourself?

What would it feel like to be able to see yourself as God sees you?

Strength for Your Day:

Today, I invite you to come just as you are and bring yourself to the word of God. Ask God to guide you to the scripture He wants you to hear. Then flip open your Bible trusting that He has led you to the place He needs you to see today. Read His word, open yourself to His word, and then you shall know yourself, as you are fully known to Him.

11

Peace & Safety

In peace I will lie down and sleep, for you alone, Lord, make me dwell in safety.

Psalm 4:8

Sleep. Some of us have a difficult time shutting down each night. We struggle with the "I need to do…," and the "I never got a chance to…," playing on repeat each night as we rest our heads down for slumber.

What happens when the brain will just not shut off? Are we doomed to forever walk each day being tired, eyes heavy, brain foggy? Or are there things we can do to obtain better sleep in our lives?

You likely know the answer to this. Yes, there are changes we can make to get better sleep in our lives. Changes to our routine, screen time, and supplements, can all help achieve better sleep. Another thing we can do is to release our thoughts to the Lord and allow Him to create the space we need for safekeeping.

God calls us to bring to Him all that we are, and all that we do. In sleep, we restore, renew, and can transform our bodies and minds. Studies continually prove the amazing power that sleep can have for us. In a much softer, more quiet way, God reminds us that He will provide a safe space in which we can rest.

Re-learning how to let myself rest was difficult for me when I was recovering from burnout. Mentally, emotionally, and physically exhausted, yet my body was in overdrive. I couldn't sit still, and if I could, my brain wouldn't sit still. Racing from thought to thought in an overactive blend of non-sense and vitally important work. I was burned out and looking everywhere else but up to find clarity.

Questions to Reflect On:

Have you ever experienced a time of burnout or stress? One in which you were in hyper-drive trying to balance all of the pieces of your life?

What would that have looked like if you had turned it all over to God and rested in the safety only He can offer? Would it have helped?

Maybe you are burned out now. What will this journey look like to recovery if you embrace God and rest your exhausted self with Him?

_____

_____

_____

_____

_____

_____

Strength for Your Day:

Today, embrace a small change in your life that will allow you to restore yourself more fully each night. Embrace giving your trust over to God. Embrace what that submission will look like for your safety, restoration, and clarity. Offer up a prayer thanking God for bringing you the peace you so desire.

12

Lead

For God, who said, "Let light shine out of darkness,"
made his light shine in our hearts to give us the light
of the knowledge of God's glory…

2 Corinthians 4:6

Have you been in the darkness? Many of us have at different times for varying reasons. In those times it is a real struggle to see the light of the knowledge of God. We tend to put our heads down in contemplation. We tend to do our best to strategize a way out of the situation, giving very little thought to God as we attempt to walk through the tough time.

The beauty of our ability to lead becomes a weakness in these moments where we try to charge through with only our earthly abilities. God's glory exists within, but we only get to glimpse it when we exercise our free will and call upon Him.

At a particularly low point in my first marriage, I can remember feeling alone. Most days, it felt like me and the kids aligned against everybody else. I remember the first time I considered leaving. I remember trying to make a plan but could never quite land on one. Packing up a small bag was the easiest part. The plan fell apart after that. There always seemed to be holes that I couldn't figure out.

I knew God didn't want us in an abusive place. I knew that I had given years waiting for things to get better, to no avail. As much as I felt like a complete failure, I knew this marriage was not the best place for the kids, or myself. I just couldn't see how to connect those dots and get us out. I had no courage. In all of the hours I spent thinking about it, I never asked God for guidance and it made the journey so much harder.

Questions to Reflect On:

Have you called upon God during your darkest times?

Or have you forsaken Him in those moments?

Do you realize the power that comes from walking with God instead of alone?

What would it/does it feel like to know you aren't alone?

Strength for Your Day:

Today, even you walk through a dark time, do you call on God? Do you realize the power that comes from walking that time with God instead of alone? Today, even if it is not a time of trial for you, call upon God to come over you, to walk this journey of life with you today and always. Ponder also, someone around you who may need this same prayer. Pray it for them, and if you get the chance, invite them to hear the message that God's light is but a prayer away.

13

Grief

Consider it pure joy, my brothers and sisters, whenever you face trials of many kinds because you know that the testing of your faith produces perseverance.

James 1:2-3

Years ago, my family and I had the privilege to know and love a wonderful man. He lost his battle with PTSD after serving our country in Afghanistan. We all entered a period of grief that I think none of us will ever fully recover from. We couldn't say, "he lived a long, happy life" when he passed. I find it's easier to deal with grief when that sentiment can be put to it, as death is a natural part of the cycle of life. His cycle, though, had been cut short.

When we were grieving it seemed like there was no end in sight. The darkness of it hovered all around us. The reminders popped up constantly as awareness began to bloom for the estimated 22 soldiers a day that our country lost to their battles with post-traumatic stress disorder at that time in our country.

Our hearts dripped with tears as the dark days stretched on. I went to see a therapist during this time who told me to practice smiling. She said, although I wouldn't feel it for some time to come, eventually I would be able to feel that smile once more. I doubted it. I practiced though. I sat in church, held back tears, and practiced my smile. I went to work and witnessed others smiling, so I practiced my smile. My children smiled, and I practiced my smile. I felt empty and numb for a very long time, but I practiced my smile.

Then one day I laughed at something silly a friend had done. I could feel that laughter bubbling within me. A small tingling sensation of something that had been dormant waking up. I felt guilty, too, for laughing when he couldn't. My friend sensed this and reminded me gently that I was alive, and that it was OK.

Sometimes our grief feels unending, a deep, dark sea of lonely despair. Our capacity to feel the loss so deeply is a testament to our capacity for love and joy. These exist as delicate dances in our lives. Sometimes heavier on one side of the room than the other, yet always swirling together.

The wisdom that comes from grief is not something that can truly be taught. We can describe it to others, but we can never impart the magnitude of such wisdom unto them. That is something that comes only with having lived through such a thing.

Questions to Reflect On:

Have you or are you facing a time of grief right now?

Are you surrounded by support? Are you struggling with it alone?

Did or do you know that this test of faith would produce inner strength gifted to you by God at this time?

What would it look like if you embraced that?

Strength for Your Day:

Today, I invite you to pray for yourself or someone else who is dealing with grief. Pray that they allow themselves to go through the process so that they, too, may once again feel the joy that God is waiting to bring into their lives.

14
Gratitude

Finally, brothers and sisters, whatever is true, whatever is noble, whatever is right, whatever is pure, whatever is lovely, whatever is admirable - if anything is excellent or praiseworthy - think about such things.

Philippians 4:8

One Thanksgiving the children and I made paper flowers to adorn the table. Pulling out orange, yellow, and brown construction paper, we cut out petals. Then we glued them onto a small wooden stick. In the center of the flower, we glued dried beans. As the family arrived for our Thanksgiving feast, we had them take a flower and write things they were grateful for on the petals. We've kept many of the flowers for the past few years. It's always fun to look back on what everyone wrote all of those years ago.

Gratitude is not a word that is unfamiliar to most of us. Often, the gratitude attitude is not a daily practice within us or within our homes. We are busy racing from one day to another. We are busy going from one "I need" to the next "I have to." We've trained our brains to race on autopilot with very little reflection on the things around us that we should feel grateful for. What happens when we stop for a moment to reflect on the things around us?

Gratitude. There is a reason why this word continues to pop up. A reason why you see coaches, psychologists, pastors, community leaders, etc… use this word often. When you practice gratitude – I mean truly practice it – your perspective shifts. Even in the darkest times, you can see light when you realize how many things you can be grateful for around you. In moments where there is no food to eat, you can be thankful that someone else isn't feeling the hunger the same way...

I practiced this one a lot some years ago. I remember praying to God and thanking Him that, though I was hungry, my children were not. I was so grateful that I had enough food to keep them well-nourished even as I went to bed with pangs of hunger gripping me. It was a dark, difficult time for us, but my children ate. We had a bed to sleep in. Small comforts around us were so much more than others had. Though it was a terrible time for us, gratitude was a daily practice within our home then as it is now.

Questions to Reflect On:

Do you practice gratitude daily?

Are you able to look around and find things to feel grateful for?

How do you think this practice will help your mindset?

Will your perspective change?

Strength for Your Day:

Today, think about or even write down some things that you are grateful for. Try to keep this practice up for the next 30 days. Reflect on what you learned during that time. What changes did you notice? What thoughts or emotions changed during this time? Offer up a prayer filled with intentional gratitude.

On getting through burnout...

"If it wasn't for my relationship with God I would never get through the times when I have been burned out. I have learned that I am trying to put things in my hand instead of God's when I get burned out. He has taught me to set boundaries. Matthew 5:37- I had to learn over time what my limits are. For example, I typically only do 2 speaking engagements that are out of state a month because more than that stresses me out."

Toni McFadden, Speaker and Author of *Redeemed, My Journey After Abortion*. ToniMcFadden.com

15

Perfect Life

Have I not commanded you? Be strong and courageous. Do not be afraid; do not be discouraged, for the Lord your God will be with you wherever you go.

Joshua 1:9

I went for a walk recently in this lovely, serene space in coastal Georgia. I walked this path nearly every morning, then again, each night during the time we stayed on Saint Simons Island, Georgia.

On this day the sun was not visible. That warm, delicious glow of early morning sunlight was hidden behind the dense fog. I walked the path, nonetheless, with my rain jacket on. The usual sounds were alive that morning. Birds chirped happily. A giant woodpecker was eagerly pecking into a couple hundred-year-old oak tree. The grounds crew was out blowing leaves, cutting grass, and prepping for the weekend. Out on the water a few sailboats sat anchored with fishing lines thrown off the back. The stillness of the water was lovely though it was hard to tell where the water ended, and the fog began.

As I walked I noticed the fog lifting. It was blowing ever so slightly to the left and up toward the sky. The sailboats became more visible. I could see pelicans and a few other birds sitting on the water, waiting to dive swiftly for their breakfast.

Sitting on a bench, I took in the beauty of the overcast morning. Even in the fog, there was immense beauty and wonder all around me. Too many times we forsake God because things are not going well. Sometimes we cannot see the beauty of the path we are on because it is covered in fog and uncertainty. We expect Him to give us a perfect journey in life, and when that doesn't happen we turn away. God doesn't promise us a perfect journey. He does tell us that if we seek Him, we will find Him. He says He will share the road with us, often carrying us through the hard times if we but place our faith in Him.

The beauty of the journey exists whether it is bathed in sunlight or hovering under dense fog. Do not let your discouragement of circumstances shake your faith, but instead, be courageous and strong.

Questions to Reflect On:

How often have you been angry with God because your path was rocky?

How often have you turned away from God because of things that have or have not happened?

Are you able to see the wonder around you even when the journey is bleak?

How do you think you would feel if you could see this perspective?

Strength for Your Day:

Today, if you have turned away from God in anger, I invite you to pray for forgiveness and ask God to continue to open your heart to His words. He is waiting to walk with you, you've only to let him know you desire to see and feel His presence once more.

16

Anxiety

When anxiety was great within me, your consolation brought me joy.

Psalm 94:19

Her tiny body was shaking ever so gently. If I hadn't been holding her, I never would have known. I jumped into action and within a few minutes, the ambulance was racing us toward the hospital. Another seizure, only this one never seemed to end. For 45 long minutes, she seized. The tiny, barely perceptible shake that thrummed through her body was so faint that I had to argue with a nurse about the fact that she was seizing at all.

If not for the fact that her face was blue no one would have listened. We spent the rest of the week in the hospital as she received every test they could throw at her. For days I barely slept. I lay there watching her each night afraid she would seize, and no one would realize it. She was just 2 years old. The fear and utter dread became a constant companion. It took me days to realize that there was a cross on the wall. Days before I even realized what color the room was. My eyes had been glued to my little girl watching, waiting for any sign of distress.

Once I noticed the cross, though, it became impossible to ignore it. My eyes would wander back and forth from my daughter to the cross. The fogginess in my brain began to lift, and I started to ramble to God. I'll never be able to remember what I said. I do know that I took deep breaths. I could sit back in the chair while she was playing in bed with her stickers. I could taste my food.

I finally slept. That cross reminded me that I could get through hard things. It reminded me that there was someone who wanted to comfort me. It reminded me that though there was great sorrow, there was also great joy. My daughter's laugh was no longer hollow. I could feel the happiness in it. I started to realize that we had the gift of alone time which we rarely got. It was just her and me for most of the day, and she seemed to be alright. There was joy as the immediate emergency began to clear a path for her health.

Feeling anxious is something that ripples through us all at different times. Some of us deal with this better than others. Yes, we still all remain empathetic about someone experiencing such an emotion. It's hard to come down from feeling anxious, especially when the trigger is still around us. Anxiety can be a very serious medical condition. If you are experiencing it I urge you to seek a trusted medical practitioner to get guidance. In addition, I remind you that God is there, ever-present, and waiting to console you with His love and strength. Sometimes we create negative habits that can aid in our anxious reactions. Peace can be cultivated, though, through mindfulness.

Questions to Reflect On:

Can you remember a time when you experienced anxiety?

Did you turn that anxiety over to God, or did you try to deal with it alone?

Reflect back on this time. What is something you can be more mindful of in the future when dealing with your own anxiety?

What is one way you can include God with you when such a time occurs?

_____

_____

_____

_____

Strength for Your Day:

Today, ask God to be with you in times when you are anxious. Ask Him to comfort you and show you the path back to joy. If this is a practice that you know well, I encourage you to offer this same prayer for someone you know who may need it at this time.

17

Faith

*Now faith is confidence in what we hope for
and assurance about what we do not see.*

Hebrews 11:1

One particularly over-cast day, I explored a beach in Coastal Georgia with a few elementary-aged children. Giant trees scattered along the shoreline which had long since lost its color, leaving in its place gorgeous driftwood. It was high tide, and the water was quite rough. Nevertheless we climbed over limbs, and under limbs as we explored laughing all the way. One of the boys noticed, "a beam of light" flashing and asked what it was.

I began to explain what a lighthouse was and was met with that wonderful, age-appropriate, "why?"

"They help guide the way for the ships. They help them know that there is land here. They can also help them find their position on a map if they have lost their way in a storm, like the one that is coming now."

After a few more back and forth exchanges, the young one lost interest in the topic and ran off to find more seashells. With the kids occupied I sat to think about this for a bit. Ship captains put such a huge amount of faith in lighthouses. Before GPS existed, there was only a map, the sunlight, the moonlight, and a compass to show the way. On a day such as this, I imagined that lives had and would be lost if one was sailing around with no lighthouse to help with positioning.

Here these towering structures stood, each one with their own history held within steadfastly shining their beacon to sailors unknown. Sailors navigating the waters now expect that beacon. They know it will light the way. There is nothing they need to do to ensure that the light shines for them. They can confidently sail forward, knowing it will shine.

What if we viewed faith in that way? A sailor is confident that the lighthouse will help guide the way even when he cannot see the way himself. He is assured that he will know of any land or danger because of its light. He is assured that by its light, he will be able to find his way once more if he is lost. He has faith in the lighthouses' ability to perform its function in order that his ship may continue to sail on. There is no guarantee of smooth waters. No guarantee of sunlight each day. No guarantee of clear days.

There is unknown in every voyage, and equal dangers lurking along the way. Yet the sailors' steadfast faith in that beacon remains unwavering, just as our faith in God should.

Questions to Reflect On:

Have you had moments when you forgot to place your faith over your fear?

Do you view God as an ever-constant lighthouse in your life, or do you only turn to Him as a last resort?

How would changing your perspective look in your life?

Strength for Your Day:

Today, ask God to come to you and remain with you steadfastly, like a lighthouse. Promise Him you will continue to trust in Him, to always lead you safely on your journey.

18

Fear & Strength

So do not fear, for I am with you; do not be dismayed, for I am your God. I will strengthen you and help you; I will uphold you with my righteous right hand.

Isaiah 41:10

Fear. Fear seems to have ruled our entire world in a very real way over the last few years. Fear of a virus. Fear of our neighbors spreading the virus. Fear of our loved ones getting a virus. Fear of gathering. Fear of being alone. Fear of science. Fear of information. Fear of control. Fear of freedom. Fear of losing freedom.

It's been everywhere, in just about everything. It's only a very lucky few who have escaped the emotion of fear over the last few years. I think it's a safe bet that we have all felt it in some way, shape, or form recently.

When I was little, I can remember a time when I went to a day camp. I had gone to the bathroom, and somehow been left behind by the group. I was walking around, trying desperately to find my way toward whatever direction they had gone off in, when I stepped on a nail that had been hidden in some leaves. It went through my foot and I immediately wailed out in pain. I remember crying out for my dad at that time, though I knew he was nowhere to be found. I was scared.

When I was afraid, my father was the one who could calm that fear. He always was, and even as an adult, he remains my strong, fierce daddy.

I remember crying and crying out for him over and over again. In all likelihood, I was probably only out in that space for about 30 minutes, but it felt like hours. I just wanted my dad there so I could borrow his strength and pretend it was my own in order to fight the pain that was radiating from my foot.

As an adult, we tend to have fewer and fewer opportunities to call upon an unassailable loved one who can strengthen us in times of need. If I had to guess, God designed it that way. As children He gives us our parents or other strong adults to help teach us lessons, to help give us strength. As adults, He wants us to look to Him to gain strength. He wants to walk with us when fear is threatening at our door. He wants to empower us through it and flex His might. Do we give Him that opportunity?

Questions to Reflect On:

Have you allowed God to walk with you in times of fear, weakness, or burden?

Have you called on Him and asked that you may gain His strength on your journey?

___

Strength for Your Day:

Today, I encourage you to pray to God and ask Him to lend His strength to your life. When you feel your fear taking hold try praying this prayer, "God, I am scared. I know you know this. I want with all my heart to turn that fear over to you. Please, help me to be able to release all of my fear and anxiety over to you. I know only you can bring me the clarity I need during this time."

19
Walk Beside Me

But you, Lord, do not be far from me. You are my strength;
come quickly to help me.

Psalm 23:19

A few months ago, we lost my father-in-law unexpectedly. He passed away with his best friend, his greatest life's joy at his side. He knew she was there, whether the stroke had altered that part of his brain or not. He knew she was there because she was always there at his side, just as he was always by hers. Fifty beautiful years they stood by one another unwavering in their commitment and love. They were the true, visible example of the way God wishes to walk with us.

Because we cannot see God in a physical way, many times we forget that He is right next to us. He will often walk softly on tiptoes so as to not disturb the things around him. Yet, He is there. He is waiting for your acknowledgment, waiting for your plea, waiting for you to say, "Hello, Lord. Thank you for walking with me today, please stay close."

It's always so much of an honor to be invited into someone's home, into their space, into their life. While God remains near you, He is eagerly awaiting that same invitation from you. Free will is something we have been gifted from Him. This means we have the ability to welcome Him in or leave the door closed.

Questions to Reflect On:

How do you choose to live today? Is it with an invitation to God to walk beside you, or with Him standing on the other side of the door?

Is it with an invitation to God to walk beside you, or with Him standing on the other side of the door?

How do you think your emotional state would change if you focused on traveling the day with God, your loving and supportive partner?

Strength for Your Day:

Today, pray openly to God and ask Him to be with you as you go through your day. Allow your prayer to fill you with the warmth that comes from walking life with a true, loving, and faithful partner. Feel the gift and strength that comes from having that kind of love surround you every moment of your day.

20
Worry

Do not be anxious about anything, but in every situation, by prayer and petition, with thanksgiving, present your requests to God.

Philippians 4:6-7

After Superstorm Sandy raged across the Northeast, we were left with nothing. We dramatically raced out of the house as the water from a broken sewage pipe gushed into our rental house, chest high. When we sat within the safety of our car as the storm raged around us, we felt grateful that we had all gotten out safely. Once it was safe enough to travel, we drove to my parent's house a few hours away. We had nothing, no place to live, no furniture, no clothes. Nothing. It was all gone, covered under whatever muck the sewage pipe had swept in.

I was so nervous as we did not have the money to buy the kids new clothes, beds, etc… I was not sure how we were going to recover.

I was afraid, tired, and overwhelmed. Yet, I was thankful to God that we had someplace safe to rest our heads. Other than that, I had no idea what we were going to do. A few hours after we arrived at my parent's house, a very close family friend arrived with bags and bags of brand new clothes for the kids.

I was overcome. The unexpected generosity was something I knew I could never repay. It was one of the most selfless things anyone had ever done for us. In my mind, it was one of the clearest moments of seeing God in action. He did not want me to be anxious. He was going to provide.

I wish I could say I truly got that lesson on that day, but it took me many years before I understood how to give things up to God in order to keep anxiety and worry at bay. Looking back, though, that was the first moment I remember seeing such a thing in action. It was a very real reflection of God's provision. It hadn't been something I petitioned directly, but it had been something I was obsessing about in my head. It was a genuine concern over the needs of my children, and I could see no way out of it without begging my family for help. Help, which they were already giving by providing a place for us to stay.

Questions to Reflect On:

Have you ever done that? Obsessed over something that you really should have just brought to God? Something you should have laid it at His feet, and asked Him to carry the burden of? Something you should have been asking Him for a solution to instead of being filled with anxiety over.

Do you think practicing this can bring you to the calm mindfulness of God's promises?

Is there something in your life currently that you are trying to handle without God's help? Reflect on it here.

Strength for Your Day:

Today, I encourage you to turn your thoughts over to God. Lift your day up to Him in prayer and ask Him to provide for anything that you may be needing. Once again, let Him know that you are working to bring your life further into His hands each and every day.

21

Restore

And the God of all grace, who called you to his eternal glory in Christ, after you have suffered a little while, will himself restore you and make you strong, firm, and steadfast.

1 Peter 5:10

My family and I all came down with Covid at the same time. One by one within a few hours we were, all five of us, sick. Our bodies felt depleted of vitamins and strength. We did what we always do when our immune system is low, we increased our fresh juice intake.

I can remember the first sip of fresh juice as it passed my lips. The flavors hit in a burst of energy as they went into my body. I knew that within fifteen minutes I would be able to feel the difference. We continued juicing and pumping in additional vitamins as our bodies slowly recovered.

While we were aware of how weak we felt, we were equally aware of how much better we felt after we drank each fresh juice. We felt restored. We knew we could count on those shots of juice to make us feel that much better.

God does this within our lives constantly. We suffer, then He restores us. We all have our own journey to travel that only God knows about. Each time we suffer and are restored, we gain strength and wisdom. That strength and wisdom are re-used again in our journey as we continue to move forward. Each time the cycle repeats, we continue to build upon the foundation that God is setting. He remains steadfast in His love for us and restores us continually.

Being open to Him and allowing Him His place within our lives allows us to see the things being done to restore us. We notice them and appreciate them with wisdom that is buried if our hearts remain closed to Him.

Questions to Reflect On:

Have you been able to see the way God has restored you after you have suffered through something?

If you have, have you taken the time to thank God for the renewal and strength He has added to your life?

If you have not been able to see the restoration within your life, what do you think that would look like?

Strength for Your Day:

Today, think about how open you have been to God. Ask that you may hear Him, and live life with Him so that you feel Him in times of suffering and know confidently that He will restore you. Think through your lifestyle and consider ways you can bring Him into your life more fully. Practice one of these ways today.

On doing too much…

"I thought that because I was a missionary, I had to help meet every need, or perceived need, that I possibly could. God played a role in everything. He helped me to learn to politely say no, even though I felt bad about it. I had much more peace and focus when I forced myself to focus on doing a few things well, instead of trying to do everything.

Tami Christianson, Mother, Blogger, Author, creator of the *Climb Mama Climb* Membership Community.

22
Faith in Action

Whatever you have learned or received or heard from me, or seen in me - put it into practice. And the God of peace will be with you.

Philippians 4:9

When I started teaching Sunday School, I set out with a theme in mind. I wanted to teach every single class, no matter what age group, how to put their faith in action. I remembered all too clearly how it felt to sit in Church each week as a kid and be talked at. I never understood what was going on. I was bored. The music was fun, but that was really the only part that got me interested. I just did not get it.

When I began teaching, I wanted the kids to walk out each week and understand what it meant to put their faith into action. I gave them different challenges each week that pertained to what we were doing. I remember being questioned when I said I was going to have them plant a seed.

"What does that have to do with the scripture?" I was asked.

I felt bad for this religious director who asked me such a question. She could not see the visual connection between the word of God, and the growth of the seeds. That week, the kids and I were discussing the importance of reading the bible…something that was not expressed to me in my childhood. I was told to memorize verses, but never taught why it was important. I was certainly never taught to just open the Bible to read it. I was talked at, not encouraged to explore and understand.

I wanted the kids to understand that when they read the Bible, their thoughts would grow the same way their seed would grow with proper care. I wanted them to understand that other people could see the seed and see the beautiful flower it was becoming. It would encourage them to take care of their own inner seeds. I wanted them to understand that reading the Bible and learning the wisdom inside would reflect on their actions and that their actions would be something other people could see. When they saw them behaving well and being kind, it would encourage others around them to do the same thing. They would be putting their faith in action.

Questions to Reflect On:

Do you put your faith in action?

Are you setting a strong, Godly example for those around you?

Have you fallen a bit off course?

Is there someone in your circle who does a good job of showing their faith in action?

Have you told them that you appreciate their example?

What is it about their example that you find uplifting and encouraging?

_____
_____
_____
_____
_____
_____

Strength for Your Day:

Today, I encourage you to give this some thought. See where you are with putting your faith in action. Put together some thoughts on how you can strengthen this within your life. The changes do not have to be large. Maybe it just means you will read a bible verse each day. Maybe it means you will find a time once a month to call a loved one who may not hear from anyone often. Think of a way you can put God's words into practice and begin adding this to your life.

23
The Pioneer

...fixing our eyes on Jesus, the pioneer and perfecter of faith. For the joy set before him he endured the cross, scorning its shame, and sat down at the right hand of the throne of God.

Hebrews 12:2

People seem to love slinging harmful words around. Maybe it was always this way, maybe it's gotten worse as frustration has spread like a disease throughout our world. It's hard to know what to say now. Hard to know what will trigger verbal attacks, or what will be well received. It's hard to understand some people's line between good and evil. Scorn. Shame. Anger. Frustration. Unhappiness. It abounds in an angry, ugly storm all around us. Just as it did for Jesus.

Yet, He remained steadfast on His path as much as He did not want the end He knew was coming. He stayed true and faithful to His Father, knowing that His journey was the redemption of us all.

The road that you are on now may be a difficult one at this time. The journey the world seems to be on is a difficult one at this time. For those of us who have set our sights on the Lord, we know that there is joy after a journey of great difficulty. We see hope, and kindness within each moment of our days. We push past fear, and offer it to God, just as Jesus did. Jesus paved the way for our path with His own. All we must do now is follow His great example. We can walk the hard road because we know the beauty of the outcome.

Questions to Reflect On:

Have you ever done something that was unpopular just because you knew it was the right thing?

Is your idea of right/wrong rooted in biblical teachings or has it adjusted to include other people's ideas instead?

When you make choices you believe are unpopular, but align with God, do you feel nervous? Afraid? Scared?

Are you worried about how others will receive it? Accept it?

What will they say? Are those voices louder than God's in your life?

Do you allow those voices to supersede God or are you a pioneer in your faith?

Strength for Your Day:

Today, may God's steady love fill you with hope and courage. May you see Jesus' example as inspiration for your own hard journey. May you know that you travel this road with love and support and that you are not alone in it. If you are not struggling, maybe you know someone who is. Offer these thoughts up to God for them.

24
God's Will

Many are the plans in a person's heart, but it is the Lord's purpose that prevails.

Proverbs 19:21

When I got married the first time, I never wanted to divorce. Throughout that 13-year marriage, through all the hardships, manipulation, and abuse, I longed for nothing more than to be able to heal my marriage and stay together. God sent Superstorm Sandy to us, and it destroyed every possession we had. When we arrived at my parent's house, I thought everything would be all right. We would be safe and stable now. We could rebuild. Then my ex got into his car and drove away. God had a purpose, though I had yet to accept it.

In my heart, I had always thought I was doing what God wanted me to be doing in my marriage. It took a natural disaster and my Ex leaving to show me otherwise. I am sure he would tell a different tale, and that is OK. It's his tale to tell. I hold no animosity toward him for the journey we traveled. The fact remains that God had a purpose that differed from the one in my heart. His purpose, once I accepted it, changed the trajectory of my life. Things were bad for a while, but once I was through it all, I could see a beauty that I had never dared imagine for myself.

In the end, no matter how hard we fight against it, God's purpose will prevail over our own. Often, the journey is much harder for us when we seek our own plans as opposed to His. Every journey comes with a lesson or lessons along the way that are vital for us to learn. Yet, learning them on God's path will always be easier than trying to learn them on our own. Prayer in all we do is the single greatest weapon we possess in aligning our lives with God's purpose for it. Remember, in all we do, at the heart of it all, God's will and not our own will should be done.

Questions to Reflect On:

How often have you asked God to help keep you on the path He has designed for you?

Have you ever tried this?

What do you think would change within your life if you turned this idea into a daily prayer?

Do you think you could see God's hand working more easily?

Do you think you will understand the greater purpose in your life?

Strength for Your Day:

Today, I invite you to think about your own journey. I invite you to ask God to put you on the path He has set for you so that you may live out His purpose for your life. If this is a prayer you are familiar with, perhaps extend the prayer out to a loved one who has not yet had the realization. Maybe even share this message with them so that they may be encouraged to try to cultivate this within their own life.

25
Refresh

Your love has given me great joy and encouragement, because you, brother, have refreshed the hearts of the Lord's people.

Philemon 1:7

Have you ever met one of those people? Someone with whom you just enjoyed their energy. Their energy made you feel warm, loved, happy, joyful? I recently went to a business retreat and met one such as this. She was radiant. It was like the sunshine was pooling out of her, spreading warmth on all of those she encountered. I was thrilled when we got a chance to talk.

Over the next few days, we had several opportunities to speak to one another. The more I spoke with Sha Sparks, the more I just enjoyed being in her company. As I voiced my adoration of her wonderful energy, she voiced hers of mine. It was a reminder of the law of attraction. In this case, our positive energies attracted us to each other. Sitting a while together left us both feeling refreshed.

Luckily, God places people here on this earth who possess this gift in order that we may understand what it feels like to be around His love. It is the briefest peek into a fraction of how we can feel when we come to have a real relationship with Him. He cannot wait to share His love with us and encircle us with His radiant joy and encouragement.

Questions to Reflect On:

Have you had an encounter with someone who has made you feel good?

Do you remember how wonderful it was, how refreshing it felt to sit within their energy?

When you spend time in prayer are you able to feel this same refreshing feeling?

What about when you join others in prayer?

Have you found a faithful community in which to share the wonderful energy of the Lord?

If you have, reflect on how that makes you feel. If you haven't, how do you think that would affect your journey with God?

Strength for Your Day:

Today, let us focus on cultivating our own positivity and pouring it outward to those around us. Allow them to feel the goodness from within you. Allow your energy to attract that goodness back from those around you. In the toughest moments of your day, ask God to come and see you through them by allowing you to radiate His love to all those you encounter.

26

Faithfulness

*Love and faithfulness meet together; righteousness and peace kiss
each other. Faithfulness springs forth from the earth
and righteousness looks down from heaven.*

Psalm 85:10-11

This verse comes alive for me every time I see my husband. Our previous spouses left us both, and we both traveled arduous journeys to find one another. I had heard about people who had found spouses that elevated their lives. Not by financial status, or materialistic possessions, but rather by being the living embodiment of God's love. I did hit a point in my life where I did not think that I was destined for such a gift. I began looking around at my friends and spiritual leaders for that example.

My husband entered my life in a gentle way, coming as a friend. He was patient, eyes shining with kindness and intelligence. He was solid in his faith, clear about his worth, or at least appeared that way when I met him. Later, I learned he was just as scared and broken as I had been, but I never saw him that way. Our courtship went slowly, as was fitting to accommodate the trauma I had been through. He never wavered in his goal to be together. I waited for him to run. I was convinced he would at any given moment.

It took many years before I relaxed into the realization that he would remain faithful to the life we created together. Through our years of marriage, my husband continues to be God's example here on earth.

Each day, regardless of what may be happening, the way he lives his life encourages me to be that same Godly example for him.

I realized I had these examples throughout my life, but never truly saw them until the wisdom clicked one day. I had parents who traveled their road together. I had friends who worked hard to be great people. I had appreciated these relationships, but I had forgotten to see God within them. I had forgotten to look for Him there. Sometimes we overlook the things that we see and are surrounded by constantly. We forget to take a step back and truly appreciate the gift of God's example all around us.

Questions to Reflect On:

Have you taken a moment to see God in the relationships around you?

Have you tried to be that wonderful, warm energy for others in your life?

What small things can you begin doing to continue to embody God's love here on earth?

Strength for Your Day:

Today, be mindful and thank God for the people He has placed around you. Call to mind the attributes they embody that you appreciate and feel grateful for in others. If you are alone, thank God for the people He will be bringing into your life. Let Him know that you are awake now and ready to receive their examples of Him. Let Him know that you realize He is there, traveling the road with you so that you are never lonely.

27
Patience

Be completely humble and gentle; be patient,
bearing with one another in love.

Ephesians 4:2

Have you ever lost your patience? I know I have. I know during times when my life was ruled by stress and anxiety, I often had a very short temper. I would snap answers back sharply, paying little attention to the person I flung them at. I would be annoyed by the mere interruption of anyone who pulled me off task. I didn't have a lot of time, I had too many things to do. That moment of interruption could set me back, and I just could not have that happen. I was short-fused, cranky, and quite honestly, I annoyed myself.

In 1 Corinthians 13:4-6, we learn what love is. It's quite a popular verse read at wedding ceremonies. It begins, "Love is patient…" Yet, patience is often the first thing we lack with our loved ones when we are stressed and tired. We see again in the above verse that we should "be patient." Depending on the version of the Bible you read from, patience is mentioned around 70 times. There is a reason for this, as I am sure scholars can explain much better than I.

I believe that it is mentioned this often for two very important reasons. One, God is a patient God, therefore, so too should we be. Two, God knows that being patient is difficult and requires practice. He knows it is hard, yet He understands its importance and significance. He calls us to rise to this challenge each and every day. He asks us to rise to that challenge in order that we will learn how to truly love, as He loves us. His love is patient.

We see examples in the Bible of God waiting long amounts of time in order to dole out consequences for bad behaviors, think of the Arc and the great flood that came. He did not rain down upon the earth for the first transgression, or even the second. He was patient. He allowed the people time to change, evolve, and come to see their errors. They did not, which ultimately caused a large consequence.

But for years, He was patient. Years… Can you imagine waiting that long to ask the co-worker next to you to chew their gum with their mouth closed? Or your neighbor to stop blowing leaves at 8 a.m. on a Saturday? Think about the massive amounts of practiced patience that would take not to get on your nerves.

Patience is learned. Patience is practiced. Patience is HARD work. Patience requires discipline.

Questions to Reflect On:

How are you with patience? Do you have it in spades?

Are you slow to anger and be annoyed?

Do you have a quick trigger in moments when you are annoyed? Interrupted?

What is a small way you can begin working on your patience with others?

What would you find difficult about this? What would you find rewarding about this?

Strength for Your Day:

Today, ask God to help you practice patience. Ask Him to carry you in those moments where you would normally be weakened. Ask Him to forgive you for the times you have not been patient. Ask Him to help you forgive yourself for your flaws and ask Him for strength as you practice loving yourself through patience with others today.

28

God Provides

So do not worry, saying, 'What shall we eat?' or 'What shall we drink?' or 'What shall we wear?' For the pagans run after all these things, and your heavenly Father knows that you need them. But seek first his kingdom and his righteousness, and all these things will be given to you as well. Therefore do not worry about tomorrow, for tomorrow will worry about itself. Each day has enough trouble of its own.

Matthew 6:31-34

I find myself constantly trying to explain to my children the difference between a "need" and a "want." We discuss patience and waiting for something versus hitting the buy now button. It's hard to teach these lessons in today's society where we all want what we want and are quick to throw things away. There is so much excess that many people rarely stop to think how much their "something old" would be valued by someone who hasn't had something new in years.

There are those of us who have lived with hunger, who have fought homelessness. Those of us who did not know where our next meal was coming from, or if we'd have a bed to sleep on from night to night. Those of us who've questioned if we could keep the heat on or the lights glowing. Those of us who wondered if the shots being fired outside would be far enough away to keep us safe. Those who've hid from banging on the door. The weight of the uncertainty of it is the kind of heavy burden that so many will thankfully never understand.

Yet for every one of those, there is one who understands all too well.

When life and circumstances have you down that low, it's hard to keep your eyes upward. It's hard not to get buried under the despair and worry that is associated with not knowing where the necessities for life will come from. This verse is meant as a reminder that God asks us to seek Him so that He may provide for the needs in our life.

Sometimes that provision is immediate, other times it takes longer. God's time is quite different from our own. Yet we are called on not to worry, but instead, bring our worry to the Lord.

Questions to Reflect On:

Do you remember to seek God in everything you do?

Are you lying awake at night worrying over things in your life? Things in society?

Are you bringing those things to God in prayer, or are you trying to control them without His help and guidance?

Strength for Your Day:

Today, I invite you to bring your burdens and worries to God. Write a list of the things you have been worrying about. Ask Him to provide for the needs of your family, for the needs you have yourself, and the needs of the world around you. Ask Him to calm your mind and release all your worry up to Him.

29

God's Attributes

But the fruit of the Spirit is love, joy, peace, forbearance, kindness, goodness, faithfulness, gentleness and self-control.

Galatians 5:22-23

In service a few weeks ago I noticed a woman. She was sitting a few rows in front of me. I noticed her because she was so incredibly joyful to be worshiping God. As we prayed and sang together, her joy and peace seemed to glow off her. It made me smile. It made me feel at peace to watch her. It brought me joy. I wanted to hug and thank her.

Service continued, and it was a deliciously deep one. Near the end of the service, I noticed her disposition had changed. Abruptly, she got up and left the room. I thought maybe she had gone to the bathroom. I waited a bit, then decided to follow. I could hear her in the bathroom sniffling. I slowly washed my hands and puttered around, killing time as I waited for her. I kept a distance when she came out, just thinking I would stay close in case she needed a friend. She stopped on her way back to the worship room. She looked so sad, I felt an overwhelming call to go to her.

I approached her slowly, "I hope you don't mind, but is everything OK?"

"Oh, that is so kind." I offered her a hug. She took some deep breaths and tried to steady herself. We pulled back from the hug, and I told her I was just going to stand beside her for a bit in case she needed a friend. She nodded and smiled through her tears. We stood in silence, staring out at the Spanish moss-covered live oak trees. Then she began to talk. She shared her thoughts with me. She thanked me for my kindness in coming over.

We chatted a bit more, then I shared my impression of her earlier. I could feel God shining within her even as she was dealing with her difficulties. Before we went our separate ways, we exchanged names. Her name was Hope.

How very fitting, I thought. She had given me hope that day just by watching her worship. Hope that I could one day shine out the attributes God gifted me in the same wonderful way she was. To me, she was the walking embodiment of this passage. Shining out love, joy, forbearance, kindness, goodness, faithfulness, gentleness, and self-control.

The story she shared with me earlier told me she had not come by these things naturally. She had worked at them all in a steadfast, strategic manner. Achieving one, then focusing on the next to cultivate all of God's glory within.

Questions to Reflect On:

Do you see the fruits of the spirit in the people in your life?

How about in your own life?

Is there one you wish to cultivate or strengthen? What is that attribute?

What do you need to do in order to get it to where you feel aligned with God in it?

Strength for Your Day:

Today, let us focus on cultivating the fruits of the spirit within ourselves so that those around us may feel God's love among them. Ask God to guide you on this journey as you strengthen your existing attributes and pursue others you may never have thought about. Ask Him to walk with you on this journey so that you can pursue these things with intention and His guidance.

30

Peace, be with you

Now may the Lord of peace himself give you peace at all times and in every way. The Lord be with all of you.

2 Thessalonians 3:16

In each day, in every way, God wishes you His peace. He wishes for you to feel His strength in every moment. He wishes for you to feel His kindness, His love, and His patience. He wishes for you to walk in this world as the embodiment of those traits. As you've now spent 29 days reflecting on His desires for your life, hopefully, you are beginning to see the power that can radiate throughout your life when you walk daily with God.

Your walk will not be perfect. We were not given this life for perfection. Your life will not be magically cured or healed. There is still work to be done whether that work is something you need to do within yourself, or it is work that God must do around you, only He knows.

You, however, can begin to heal from the anxious, stressed out, and exhausted path you have been on. There are more changes to make, but having God alongside you in this journey has added a power that was not there before. It has added a place to restore and fill you up once more with the grace and love that only He can provide.

Questions to Reflect On:

Have you been able to see the power of God working within your life over the last 29 days?

Have you felt a difference in the way you have lived each day knowing He was there with you?

Now that you have created this new habit of walking with God, how do you plan to continue to prioritize it daily?

Strength for Your Day:

Today and all the days following, I invite you to pray with me. Join me each morning in praying for God's constant presence throughout your day. Join me as we ask for help for our weaknesses. Join me as we ask that God allows us to be His example here on earth. Remember to take this time for yourself. Do it in the quiet of the morning, in the car, or in the shower. Wherever you can carve out a moment to speak to Him, I invite you to continue to do so. Congratulations on achieving 30 days of prayer, it is but the beginning to cultivating the clarity and significance you wish to regain in your life.

On the worst part of burnout...

"The worst part was feeling like I was the only one in the world who has felt this way. Feeling like I was isolated and alone and that no one would understand. Also, I felt overwhelmed by all the things that lay in front of me and I didn't know what to do next. I was frozen in procrastination perfection and analysis paralysis. What if I make the wrong choice? These fears had me not making any progress because I couldn't decide which thing had the most priority. All of them had priority."

On giving it over to God...

"When I was stuck in fear mode and listening to the enemy of analysis paralysis, I wasn't praying and asking for support. I was trying to control things in my own way instead of surrendering it all to Him and leaning on Him to provide me with the next step. If anything, my past has taught me that I have no control and that when I ask for support, I receive it. When I pray for the next step, oftentimes, a new door opens that I wasn't even aware of before. When I walk through that door with zero expectations and ask God, who am I supposed to meet, what am I supposed to learn, and will you speak through me, that is when the true curious exploration of God's light shows up in my life. The blessing shines in the surrender."

Sha Sparks, Chief Excitement Officer of Sparks of Fire International and host of *The Power of Investing in People* podcast. ShaSparks.com

About the Author

M.J. James is a coach, speaker, and first-time author from the Golden Isles, Georgia. She has an online platform that empowers clients to embrace clear, balanced paths in life and business.

Let's Connect

✉ mj@mjjames.com

🌐 MJJames.com

facebook.com/mjjamesofficial

linkedin.com/in/mjjamesauthor

My most sincere thanks to the following people for giving feedback, encouragement, and support during the creation of this book:

Antoinette Chiarello	Kent Sanders
Desiree Thurston	Mary Boza Crimmins
Greg Gerber	Melissa Jergenson
Jennifer Harshman	Sarah Geringer
Katlynn Pyatt	Terri Tonkin

Additional Resources

Looking for some resources on dealing with burnout?

Check out my website **MJJames.com** or scan the QR code below for a **FREE Burnout Recovery Workbook.**

www.ingramcontent.com/pod-product-compliance
Lightning Source LLC
Chambersburg PA
CBHW032039040426
42449CB00007B/945